Grandmother Isabella's First

Isabella Ann Cale (Nee Langlois)

Isabella was born at 25 Seaton Place, St Helier, Jersey, Channel Islands on the 31st December 1886.

Married to Robert Joseph Cale in St Peters Church, West Hackney, London on the 23rd September 1916. She died from a stroke in Ouseley Road Hospital, Balham, London on the 14th June 1933, aged 46.

Isabella collected most of the recipes from friends and colleagues in France during the First World War whilst she was an interpreter, speaking fluent French, for the American Embassy in Paris.

After the war she collated all the 'receipts' (as she called them), into a recipe note book during 1919 in London whilst pregnant with her daughter.

The book was given to her daughter, Joan Isabella Whittaker (nee Cale) who was born on the 29th March 1920 in Hackney, London. Joan moved to Jersey with her family in 1955 and has lived there ever since. Joan then passed the book onto her daughter Ann Le Galle (nee Whittaker). Ann was born on 26th September 1952 in Bromley, Kent and has also lived in Jersey since 1955.

This book was compiled by:
Isabella's Granddaughter, **Ann Le Galle** (nee Whittaker)

(The book is as close to the original copy as possible).

(Some imagination may be required!)

There are no pictures, and the majority of recipes are very basic, so a little imagination at times will be required.

The book I believe will be fun for children to try. They will have the anticipation of seeing the results and knowing that this is the food from 100 years ago. (Some recipes not so different from today!)

A few tips:

- When frying Liver, dip each piece in milk, it will fry a deep rich brown and will not be hard.

- If bacon is soaked in water for 3 or 4 minutes before frying it will prevent grease from running and give it a much finer flavour.

- Ham and Bacon are much better cooked in the oven than on the top of the range and there is less danger of them burning. The meat will be beautifully brown and the fat in the pan clearer than when fried as usual.

- When frying Rissoles or Fish Cakes put a teaspoonful of vinegar into the frying fat. This prevents the cakes from being too greasy when cooked.

- Old Potatoes frequently turn black when boiled. If a few drops of vinegar are added to the water in which they are cooked they will be quite a good colour.

- I believe that in the ingredients of the recipes that have 'flour' in them it was Plain flour.

This name was at the back of the note book that Isabella had written her recipes in. It is her Brother, Harold Langlois. He lived at Victoria House, Beaumont, St Peter, Jersey. The house is still there today.

H Langlois 516310
R. E. Signal
20th Division
France

This recipe book was finished and printed in 2015.

Biscuits

Home Made Gingerbread

Ingredients

1 lb of flour
6 ozs butter
4 ozs sugar
2 ozs candied peel
¾ oz ground ginger
1 teaspoonful of mixed spice
1 teaspoonful of carbonate of soda
1 egg
4 teaspoonfuls of treacle

Method

Cut up the candied peel.
Mix with the ginger, spice and flour.
Beat the butter and sugar to a cream.
Add the egg and treacle.
Mix in the dry ingredients except for the soda which should be dissolved in a little milk then added.
Cook in a slow oven for about two hours and be careful that the oven is kept at a moderate heat.

American Crackers

Ingredients

1¾ lbs of flour
½ lb lard
½ oz of bicarbonate of soda
½ oz baking powder
3 Gills milk
½ lb chopped raisins or dates

Method

Sieve the chemicals into the flour.
Rub the lard in.
Add to milk.
Add the fruit and mix up to a firm paste.
Roll it out thinly, cut pieces with a round cutter.
Dock over with a fork.
Place on oven tray not too close together and bake in a moderate over.

Tips:
Chemicals = Bicarbonate of soda and baking powder
1 Gill = 5 fluid ozs or 142 ml
Dock = (Prick)

Fairy Biscuits

Ingredients

1 lb of flour
½ lb rice flour or ground rice
12 ozs margarine
4 ozs sugar
½ oz cream of tartar
4 ozs currants or raisins or chopped dates
A gill of milk

Method

Sieve the powders into the flour.
Cream up the fat and sugar.
Add the milk, stir it in well.
Then add the flour and rice and fruit.
Mix the whole up to a soft batter.
Drop the batter on greased tins with a spoon.
Give them room to flow and bake in a hot oven.

Tip:
1 Gill = 5 fluid ozs or 142 ml

Chocolate Macaroons

Ingredients

2 eggs
½ lb of castor sugar
1 lb of desiccated cocoanut
¼ lb of plain chocolate
Icing sugar

Method

Whip the whites of the eggs to a solid froth.
Stir in half pound of castor sugar.
Then add desiccated cocoanut.
(A very crumbly mixture is generally the result of this)
Then this should be shaped into little balls or cones and put on a well buttered tin to dry in the oven until they stay in shape without breaking.
They will require about 20 minutes to bake in an oven that is not too hot.
Melt the plain chocolate with a very little water.
Stir in a little icing sugar and with this mixture coat each macaroon.

Lemon Puffs

Ingredients

4 tablespoonfuls of butter
1 cupful of water
1 cupful of flour
Pinch of salt and one teaspoonful of sugar
4 eggs

Method

Into a small saucepan put the butter.
Add one cupful of water, bring to boiling point.
Add quickly one cupful of flour, pinch of salt and the sugar.
Cook and stir well with a wooden spoon until the mixture leaves the sides of the pan.
Take from the fire, allow to cool, but not become cold.
Add eggs, beating each one in thoroughly.
Set away in a cool place for one hour and a half.
Drop in spoonfuls on a greased baking tin.
Brush with beaten egg, sprinkle with chopped nuts.
Bake in a hot oven for thirty minutes.
When cold split them open on one side and fill them with lemon filling and a spoonful of whipped and sweetened cream.

Napolitains

Ingredients

½ lb flour
4 ozs ground almonds or cocoanut
4 ozs sugar
4 ozs butter or margarine
1 egg

Method

Rub the butter and almonds together.
Then rub in the flour and sugar.
Mix up to a paste with the egg.
Roll out thin.
Cut out pieces with a round cutter and put them on greased tins.
Bake in a cool oven.
When baked place two together with jam and dredge the tops with sugar.

Monte Cristo's

Ingredients

3 ozs ground almonds or cocoanut
4 ozs sugar
2 eggs
2 ozs butter or margarine
1 oz flour.

Method

Beat up the eggs, sugar and almonds or cocoanut.
Add the butter, melted, and then add the flour.
Mix up to a soft mass and put spoonfuls in small fancy square tins.
Bake them in a cool oven.
When done dip the tops in a little rum, then into sugar and place half an almond in the centre.

Bresils

Ingredients

10 ozs flour
10 ozs butter
4 ozs ground almonds or cocoanut
4 ozs sugar
2 egg yolks
A little cinnamon

Method

Rub the butter into the flour.
Add the sugar and almonds and spice.
Mix up to a stiff paste with the egg yolks.
Then roll the paste out to ½ inch in thickness and cut into strips
2 inches wide, the length of the tin to be used.
Bake in a hot oven.
When done and while warm cut each strip in two.
Spread jam on one piece, lay another piece on the top dredge with
sugar and cut up into suitable pieces.

Short Cake

Ingredients

½ lb butter
1 lb flour
1 large egg
¼ lb caster sugar.

Method

Rub the butter in the flour.
Then add the sugar and mix into a paste with the beaten egg.
Roll out and cut into rounds or squares.
Put on to floured tins and lay a slice of candied citron on the top.
Cook in slow oven.

Parisian Cream Cigarettes

Ingredients

5 eggs
½ lb sugar
½ lb flour

Method

Whisk up the eggs and sugar.
Then gently stir the flour in to make a very soft batter.
Drop a spoonful on papered tins.
Bake in a hot oven.
When done roll each one round a lead pencil or holder.
Then gently take the stick out and fill the cases with butter cream.
Another way is to spread the cream on the sponge cake and then fold up as would be done with a Swiss roll, but they are generally rolled on sticks.
A little cocoa powder may be added to the eggs when beating up thus making the cakes a dark colour.
Fill the centre with cream and then roll them in fine cocoanut.

Raspberry Croquettes

Ingredients

Raspberries
Sugar and water
1 lb of fine breadcrumbs
Nut butter
Egg and breadcrumbs

Method

Slice the raspberries gently in a syrup of sugar and water until cooked.
Strain off the juice.
Beat up the fruit and stir in the fine breadcrumbs.
Add sufficient of the juice to make the whole a very stiff paste.
Spread on a dish to cool.
Have ready a pan with some boiling nut butter.
Form the mixture into convenient pieces and coat with the egg and breadcrumbs.
The pieces should then be fried until they are a nice brown.

Cheese Straws (Jersey)

Ingredients

2 ozs flour
Pinch of salt and cayenne pepper
1 spoonful of red pepper
3 ozs of parmesan cheese
2 ozs of butter
Yolk of an egg

Method

Take the flour and mix with it a little salt, cayenne and the red pepper.
Then grate the parmesan cheese and add to mixture.
Rub the cheese and butter well into the flour mixture.
Mix all these ingredients together with the yolk of an egg into a smooth stiff paste.
Roll the paste out into a strip one eighth of an inch in thickness and five inches wide which is to be the length of the cheese straws.
With the remainder of the paste and with two round cutters cut little rings of paste.
Put cheese straws and rings on the baking sheet and put them into a hot oven for 10 minutes.
The heat rising to 246 degrees.
For serving put the cheese straws through the rings (like a bundle of sticks).

Bread

Milk Breakfast Rolls

Ingredients

A pint and half of milk quite warm
A quarter pint of brewers yeast
6 ozs of butter
1 oz of sugar
3 Eggs

Method

Mix well together in a pan with sufficient flour to make a thick batter.
Let it stand in a warm place covered over until it is well risen.
Melt the butter, add sugar to the butter.
Then break the eggs into the pan.
Mix them well together and add sufficient flour to make it into a dough.
Let it stand for ¼ of hour and then work it up again.
Then break into pieces large or small and roll them round smooth with the hand.
Make a small hole in the centre of each.
Place them in a cooking tin and cover with a piece of thick flannel.
Put in a warm place to prove them.
A quick oven is the best for baking.

Vienna Bread

Ingredients

1½ lb flour and half a teaspoonful of salt
1 oz of German yeast
1 Dessert spoonful of sugar
2 ozs butter
1 breakfast cupful and a half of milk
1 egg

Method

Into a warmed basin put the flour and half a teaspoonful of salt.
Then into a small bowl place German yeast and mix it with the sugar.
Beat these two ingredients until they resemble a liquid.
Melt in a small pan the butter and milk.
(Care being taken that the mixture is not allowed to gel beyond a lukewarm temperature).
The butter and milk are then added to the beaten yeast and sugar.
Drop the egg into centre of the flour and mix a little.
Then add the liquid ingredients beating all well with a wooden spoon.
Sprinkle a little flour over the dough cover the basin with a lid and set the dough to rise in a warm place for one hour and half.
Then turn the dough on to a floured board, knead and roll into a long piece.
Cut into strips and form them into twists.
Next place the loaves onto a floured oven shelf and again set them to rise in a warm place for 10 minutes.
Bake for 15 minutes.

Milk Rolls

Ingredients

1 lb flour
1 oz butter
1 oz yeast
A little milk and salt

Method

Warm the milk and dissolve the yeast in it with the salt.
Then rub the butter into the flour.
Make a hole in the centre, pour in the milk and yeast and mix to a stiff dough.
Cover the bowl and leave in a warm place.
When it is well risen turn onto a board and knead well.
Cover bowl again and leave for a time.
Flour a baking tin.
Form the dough into small rolls then cover and leave again for 20 minutes.
Brush tops of rolls with beaten egg and then bake in a quick oven.

War Time Short Paste

Ingredients

1 lb flour
½ lb margarine
Little salt
A gill of water

Method

Rub the margarine into the flour adding a little salt and mix the whole up to a paste with the water. Handle it lightly.
Roll it out and use as desired.

Tip:
1 Gill = 5 fluid ozs or 142 ml

Cakes

Cocoanut Rocks

Ingredients

1 lb of flour
4 ozs cocoanut
½ oz of cream of tartar
¼ oz bicarbonate of soda
6 ozs margarine
½ lb moist sugar
2 eggs
½ pint milk

Method

Sieve the 'chemicals' into the flour rub the margarine in finely.
Then mix in the cocoanut.
Make a hollow in the middle and insert the sugar.
Add the beaten eggs and the milk and mix the whole up to a cake batter.
Spoon out onto greased tins.
Then dredge over with a little sugar to which a little cocoanut has been mixed.
Each cake should be about 1 oz and ¾.
But if the eggs are left out they become a little larger.

Tips:
'Chemicals' = Bicarbonate of Soda and Cream of Tartar
'Moist' sugar = (slightly moistened with water)

Hot Cross Buns

Ingredients

1 lb flour
1 cup full of lukewarm water
½ teaspoonful of ground ginger
½ teaspoonful of allspice
2 tablespoonfuls of sugar
A good pinch of salt
½ oz to 1 oz of yeast.

Method

Mix the yeast with one teaspoonful of flour, one teaspoonful of sugar and two tablespoonfuls of lukewarm water.
Sift the dry ingredients into a warm basin.
Make a well in the centre of the flour.
Pour in the yeast, adding lukewarm water.
Stir with a wooden spoon into a light dough.
Knead well until the dough no longer sticks to the basin.
Turn smooth side up and stand to rise in a warm place for one hour.
Divide into small portions.
Cut an X on top of each.
Leave to rise for 15 minutes in a warm place and bake in a hot oven.
4 tablespoonfuls of currants or seedless raisins may be added and the spice omitted if desired.

Queen Cakes

Ingredients

3 ozs butter
3 ozs sugar
2 eggs
6 ozs flour
3 ozs currants
1 teaspoonful of baking powder

Method

Cream together butter and sugar, add eggs and the flour.
Beat well.
Then add the raisins and baking powder.
Pour the mixture into small greased tins and brown nicely in the oven.

Aerated Tea Cakes

Ingredients

1½ lb flour
½ lb cornflour or rice flour
6 ozs margarine
3 ozs sugar
3 ozs currants
1 oz cream tartar or substitute
½ oz of bicarbonate of soda
½ pint milk and ½ pint water

Method

Mix the two flours together and sieve the powders in.
Rub the margarine and sugar in.
Add the currants and mix the whole up to a smooth paste with the milk and water.
Roll it out with the rolling pin to about ½ inch thick.
Cut out rounds the size of a muffin plate, four inches across.
Wash over with water and bake in a hot oven.
Dates or figs may be used.
Will keep moist for days.

West Indian Cake

Ingredients

¼ lb butter
½ lb flour
½ gill milk
2 small eggs
2 ozs fine sugar
2 ozs orange peel
4 ozs currants
Rind of ½ lemon
½ teaspoonful baking powder
A little grated nutmeg.

Method

Rub the butter in the flour and add the sugar.
Then add the milk which should be boiling.
The eggs well beaten, the lemon rind grated, nutmeg, currants wash dried and picked.
Peel finely and chop.
Add baking powder mix thoroughly.
Put into a buttered and papered cake tin and bake in a good hot oven for about an hour.

Tip:
1 Gill = 5 fluid ozs or 142 ml

Jersey Wonders

Ingredients

7 eggs
3 lb bag of flour
7 ozs butter
2 cups sifted sugar
A little lemon grated
Nutmeg
Plenty of lard to boil them

Method

Rub butter into flour and sugar.
Whisk eggs and add to mixture.
Add grated lemon and nutmeg.
Roll out on floured board to ⅙th of an inch thick using as little flour
as possible, cut into sausage shapes.
Cut slits in middle and turn ends inside through slit.
Heat the lard in large deep pan until smoking hot and cook the
Wonders until golden brown.
Lift out and drain.

Rolleaux

Ingredients

6 ozs ground almonds or cocoanut
4 eggs
½ lb sugar
4 ozs melted butter
2 ozs finely minced orange peel
2 ozs flour.

Method

Beat up the eggs.
Then add the sugar and almonds or cocoanut, beating all the time.
Then add the melted butter beating well in.
Add the peel and flour and mix lightly.
Spoon out on to greased tins and bake in a cool oven.
When done press together with jam.

Tea Scones

Ingredients

1 lb self raising flour
¼ lb lard
¼ lb sugar.

Method

Mix the lard, sugar and flour together and add milk to make a firm paste.
Roll out ¼ in thick and cut with a cutter.
Cook in a moderate over.

Sud Cake

Ingredients

4 ozs butter
Teaspoonful of baking powder
8 ozs flour
6 ozs moist sugar
½ oz caraway seed
1 egg
Pinch salt
A little milk to mix.

Method

Rub the butter into the flour.
Add the sugar, seeds, baking powder and salt and mix well.
Beat up the egg, add a little milk to it, and stir into mixture.
Pour into a buttered cake tin and bake one hour in a moderately heated oven.

Tip:
'Moist' sugar = (slightly moistened with water)

Cocoanut Diamonds

Ingredients

8 ozs flour
3 ozs cocoanut
3 ozs sugar
4 ozs butter
2 eggs
Teaspoonful baking powder

Method

Cream together the butter and sugar.
Add the eggs well beaten, and two teaspoonfuls of milk.
Beat for a few minutes then gently stir in the flour and afterwards add the baking powder and cocoanut.
Pour the mixture into a buttered tin and bake quickly.
When sufficiently baked allow to cool.
Then cut into diamond shapes and put cocoanut icing on each.

Coffee Cakes

Ingredients

4 ozs butter
4 ozs sugar
½ lb sifted flour
6 ozs plumped currants
A little milk
Baking powder
2 eggs
Strong cold coffee

Method

After beating together the butter and sugar stir in gradually the sifted flour.
Mix well beaten eggs and a little milk.
Add currants.
Make a small quantity of strong coffee.
When cool add a good tablespoonful to the mixture.
Then mix in a heaped teaspoonful of baking powder.
Put into greased tins and bake in a brisk oven for 15 mins.
While warm they should be iced with coffee flavoured icing.

Currant Buns

Ingredients

1 cup and half of warm sweet milk.
1 cup sugar
1 cup yeast
½ cup butter
1 cup currants
Flour

Method

Make a stiff batter, let it rise overnight.
In the morning stir in as much flour as possible with a spoon.
Let it rise again and bake in a quick oven.
Sometimes it is preferred to stir in a beaten egg with the flour.

Fruit Cake

Ingredients

9 ozs self raising flour
5 ozs butter
5 ozs castor sugar
2 ozs each of glace cherries, candied lemon peel,
blanched and split almonds and currants
1 oz of sultanas
3 eggs and a little milk

Method

Beat together the butter and sugar.
Beat up eggs in a separate basin.
Mix in the eggs and flour alternately with the butter and sugar, half of
the cherries and lemon peel.
Mix well together adding the currants last.
Pour into a tin and bake in a moderate oven for an hour.

Cinnamon Fruit Cake

Ingredients

1 cupful of brown sugar
1 well beaten egg
A piece of butter the size of an egg
1 cupful of sour cream
1 teaspoonful of soda
1 teaspoonful of cinnamon
½ a nutmeg grated
2 cupfuls of flour and 1 cupful and a half of stoned raisins

Method

Not given. (Imagination needed!)

Cocoanut Rocks

Ingredients

1 lb flour
6 ozs fine cocoanut
6 ozs margarine
6 ozs sugar
½ oz cream of soda
4 ozs lemon peel cut fine
½ pint milk

Method

Sift the powders into the flour.
Rub the margarine in well.
Add the cocoanut and peel, cut fine.
Then mix the whole up to a nice dough.
The milk is sufficient.
Divide into 16 pieces 2¾ oz each.
Roll up round, put on tins and with a fork break up into a rough cake.
Wet the tops with milk, dust with sugar and bake in hot oven.

Currant Teacakes

Ingredients

1 lb of flour
3 teaspoonfuls of baking powder
½ pint milk
½ teaspoonful of salt
¼ lb currants or sultanas

Method

Melt the butter in the milk and pour the mixture over the flour, baking powder and salt which should have been put in a large bowl. When the dough is made add the currants and divide the dough into small pieces.
Shape them into buns and bake on a greased tin in a hot oven.

Chocolate Rock Cakes

Ingredients

Teaspoonful of baking powder
1½ lb flour
2 ozs cornflour.
2 ozs butter
2 ozs chocolate powder
1 egg
Cold coffee

Method

Mix baking powder, flour and cornflour together.
Rub in butter and chocolate powder and the well beaten egg.
Make into a soft dough with strong cold coffee.
Divide into small cakes and bake in patty tins.

Choice Fruit Cake

Ingredients

1 lb flour
¼ lb lard or dripping
½ lb sugar
¼ lb sultanas
½ lb currants
1 teaspoonful of carbonate of soda
A gill of sour milk or butter mild

Method

Rub dripping or lard in the flour add the fruit and sugar.
When these are mixed stir soda into the milk and mix with the other ingredients.
Bake in a moderate oven for two or two and half hours until a rich brown colour has been obtained.

Tip:
1 Gill = 5 fluid ozs or 142 ml

Arrowroot Cakes

Ingredients

14 ozs of flour
2 ozs of cornflour
½ lb of arrowroot
½ lb margarine
6 ozs of sugar
½ oz cream of tartar substitute
¼ oz of bicarbonate of soda
½ pint milk
A gill water
Essence of lemon

Method

Sieve the flour, cornflour, arrowroot and the chemicals together.
Rub the margarine and sugar in it and mix the whole up to a cake
batter with the milk and water.
Fill into large papered tins and bake in a hot oven or it can be baked in
small patty tins.

Tips:
Gill = 5 fluid ozs or 142 ml
'Chemicals' = Bicarbonate of Soda and Cream of Tartar

Cocoanut Cake

Ingredients

1 lb flour
4 ozs butter
6 ozs sugar
2 eggs

Method

Rub the butter and sugar well into the flour. Make a hollow.
Add the eggs beaten up and mix to a rather stiff paste with a little milk.
Roll out to one eighth of an inch and a half in diameter or any size required.
Place on baking tins then make up the following:
½ lb fine cocoanut
½ lb fine castor sugar
2 ozs ground rice
1 egg.
Mix the sugar, cocoanut and ground rice together and mix up to a stiff paste with egg.
Roll out thin and cut rings out of it half the size of the biscuits.
Place one on top of each biscuit and then bake.

Cornish Cake

Ingredients

6 ozs of lard
1 lb of flour
3 ozs of brown sugar
6 ozs currants
A few pieces of candied peel
Milk

Method

Rub the lard into the flour.
Add the brown sugar, currants and a few pieces of candied peel, (cut small), and enough milk to make a rather stiff paste.
Roll out to three quarters of an inch thick and bake on well greased tin for half hour.
Bake in a moderate oven.

Genoese Cake

Ingredients

3 eggs
4 ozs of caster sugar
A teaspoonful of fine very dry flour.
Butter

Method

Beat the eggs and caster sugar in a basin over a saucepan of boiling water until they thicken, about 12 to 15 minutes.
Put the basin on the table.
Add a piece of butter the size of an egg approx (3 ozs), previously warmed.
Add liquid and finally stir in as lightly as possible.
Add the fine very dry flour.
Bake quickly in a paper lined buttered shallow tin calculated to produce a cake about two inches thick.

Sunderland Cake

Ingredients

½ lb of flour
¼ lb of butter
2 ozs of sugar
¼ lb of golden syrup
6 ozs currants
3 eggs
1 teaspoonful of baking powder
Fruit (imagination needed) **

Method

Take the flour, put through a sieve.
Mix the powder well with the flour and beat thoroughly together.
Mix in the currants.
Beat the butter and sugar to a cream.
Add the syrup after it is slightly heated.
Whisk the eggs, yokes and whites separately and after adding the yolks beat well and stir in whites.
Have fruit ready picked and cleaned and stir in the mixture thoroughly. **
Pour into a greased tin and bake in a moderate oven for about an hour and a half.

Tip:
To make a cake light add a few drops of glycerine.
When mixing in the proportions of a teaspoonful to a pound of flour.

Substantial Tea Cake

Ingredients

1 lb of flour
½ lb of beef suet
¼ lb of butter
½ lb currants
¼ lb of peel
6 ozs sugar
2 teaspoonfuls of baking powder
Small quantity of milk

Method

Mix the flour, baking powder, half a teaspoonful of salt, sugar, butter, currants and peel.
Then add the shredded suet.
Add sufficient milk to make a stiff paste.
Turn on a slightly floured board or slab, roll out to a thickness of about half an inch.
Bake in a quick oven and serve hot, cut into diamonds.

Tip:
1 Gill = 5 fluid ozs or 142 ml

Surprise Cake!!
(There is no title to this recipe)
Good luck with it and be surprised at the outcome!!

Ingredients

Small teacupful of milk
2 ozs of butter
1 beaten egg
¾ lb of dry and slightly warm flour mix
Small teaspoonful of salt
1 oz of compressed yeast and a teaspoonful of sugar

Method

In a saucepan beat well together the butter with the milk and this should be well beaten together.
Then add the beaten egg, taking care to have the whole no more than lukewarm.
With the dry and slightly warm flour mix a small teaspoonful of salt.
Stir together till liquid.
Add the compressed yeast and a teaspoonful of sugar.
Then add the contents of the saucepan.
Mix this with the flour and knead until quite smooth.
Divide into two equal portions.
Form these into round cakes and place them in greased round tins.
Keep them near the fireside for about an hour.
Then bake them in a fairly hot oven.
Brush them over with sugar dissolved in a very small amount of water when nearly done.

Scones

Ingredients

½ lb self raising flour
½ teaspoonful baking powder
½ a breakfast cupful sour milk
1½ ozs margarine
Pinch of salt

Method

Weigh the flour and add margarine, salt and baking powder.
Mix well together then add sour milk.
Bake in moderate oven for about 20 minutes.
Roll out an inch thick.

Fruit Cake

Ingredients

11 ozs self raising flour
8 ozs margarine
6 oz castor sugar
2 or 3 eggs
Lemon rind or any flavouring

Method

Mix together margarine and the sugar.
Beat in the eggs.
Add lemon rind or flavouring.
Fold in the flour.

Tip:
No fruit was suggested (imagination needed)

Jam Sandwiches

Ingredients

Bicarbonate of Soda
Cream of tartar
2 ozs flour
4 ozs butter
4 ozs caster sugar
4 ozs desiccated cocoanut

Method

Mix a pinch of bicarbonate of soda and cream of tartar with the flour.
Work together until smooth.
Add the butter and caster sugar.
Then beat in eggs adding part of the flour with each one.
Stir in the remainder of the flour and desiccated cocoanut.
Bake in two sandwich tins.
When cool spread between cakes any jam.

Suet and Jam Roly-Poly

Ingredients

3 ozs Suet
½ lb of flour
Pinch of salt
½ teaspoonful baking powder
Water

Method

Chop the suet finely and mix with the flour and a pinch of salt and the baking powder.
Add sufficient water to mix to a stiff dough and form into a roly-poly spreading with jam.
2 hours for boiling.

Swiss Cheesecakes

Ingredients

Short pastry
Some strawberry, raspberry or apricot jam
1 good tablespoonful of fine sugar
A piece of butter half the size of an egg
1 egg
½ teacup of flour
1 teaspoonful of baking powder
A good pinch of salt

Method

Line a number of tartlet tins with short paste.
In each tin place a little strawberry, raspberry or apricot jam.
Beat together with a wooden spoon until thick and creamy the fine sugar and the piece of butter.
Then work in an egg.
Mix the flour with the baking powder and a good pinch of salt and stir them lightly into the other ingredients.
Give each tin an equal portion of the mixture.
Bake for about half an hour in a quick oven.

Drinks

Ginger Wine

Ingredients

5 Drahms ginger
1 Drahm capsieum
1 Drahm lemon
6 Drahms burnt sugar
1 oz Tartaric acid

Method

No method given (Imagination needed!)

Tips:
1 Drahm = 1/8 of a fluid ozs or (3.70 mls)
Burnt sugar = (Place sugar on tray and place in oven until brown)

Lemonade

Ingredients

2 pints of water
2 lbs sugar
1 oz citric acid
1 Drahm of essence of lemon

Method

Boil the water and sugar for 15 minutes. Let it cool.
Mix acid and lemon.
Bottle for use.

Tip:
1 Drahm = 1/8 of a fluid oz or (3.70 mls)

Odds

Tripe

Ingredients

2 lbs tripe
¼ lb bacon
Herbs
6 cloves
Pepper and salt,
Onion
Carrots
Cauliflower foot
¼ lb pork skin

Method

Wash in cold water the tripe.
Put in crock with water.
Add the bacon cut in small pieces.
Add the herbs, cloves, pepper, salt, onion, carrots, and cauliflower foot.
Add pork skin, pinch of nutmeg and the water or broth.
Takes about 7 hours to cook.
When cooked pour in a glass of cognac.

Lemon Marmalade

Ingredients

12 Lemons
Water
1½ lb sugar per pound weight of lemons

Method

Wash and dry the lemons and weigh them whole.
Put them into a pan cover with cold water enough to float them.
Cook steadily until they can be easily pierced. They may require from one to two hours.
When tender slice them thinly removing seeds and hard pieces.
Now measure the water in which they cooked and make up the quantity required.
One pint to each pound weight of lemons.
Put fruit, sugar and water in a preserving pan and cook steadily until the juice 'jellies' on a place when cold.
Stir often and keep well skimmed.
Put into dry jars and when cold tie down.

Salad Mayonnaise

Ingredients

1 tablespoonful vinegar
1 tablespoonful oil
½ tablespoonful milk
Pinch of salt
1 yolk egg

Method

Warm up together over the gas ring until it thickens.
Then add a knob of butter a little mustard or mustard from pickles,
fish paste or any other.

Home Made Chutney

Ingredients

½ lb of sultanas
¼ lb of raw sugar
½ lb of sour apples
½ oz of garlic
1 oz of mustard seed
1 teaspoonful of salt
1 large tomato
1 banana
1½ pints vinegar

Method

Chop all the ingredients as fine as possible.
Then boil the whole in the vinegar very gently for 4 hours until it becomes the thickness of jam.
When cold it is ready for use.

Cold Meat Cutlets

Ingredients

½ lb of any cold meat
½ lb of cooked potatoes
2 teaspoonfuls each of chopped parsley and onion
1 teaspoonful of salt, 1 pinch of pepper
1 egg + yolk of an egg
White crumbs
Parsley

Method

Finely cut the cold meat.
Rub the cooked potatoes through a sieve.
Mix together with the meat, potato, chopped parsley and onion.
Add the salt and pepper.
Beat up the egg yolk and add it to the mixture.
If it is too stiff add a little stock.
Smooth the mixture evenly on a plate and mark it with a knife into even divisions.
Work each division into a cutlet shape.
Brush them over with a beaten egg and cover them with white crumbs.
Have ready a pan of frying fat.
When a bluish smoke rises from it put in 2 or 3 at a time and fry until a golden brown.
Drain well on kitchen paper.
A small piece of parsley should be put on the top of each before they are served hot.

Mint Sauce for Lamb

Ingredients

Fresh mint
Powdered sugar
3 tablespoonfuls of vinegar

Method

Strip the leaves from the fresh mint.
Wash and dry them well and chop them as finely as possible.
Put them into a tureen and cover them with the powdered sugar. (The proportion of a tablespoonful of sugar to one and a half of mint).
Let these remain for ½ hour.
Then pour vinegar over them.
If after a trial this sauce is found to be too sweet less sugar can be used.

Scalloped Fish

Ingredients

Any variety of fish
Brown breadcrumbs
Parsley
Butter
1 Egg
Salt and Pepper
Chopped Parsley

Method

Scrape the fish from the bone and skin and flake it.
Then allow a third the amount of fish in breadcrumbs (browned).
Season with salt and pepper.
Then add the egg boiled hard and chopped.
Mix all together.
Form into scallop-shaped pieces or fill the shells with the mixture after
they have been buttered.
Place them in a moderate oven with a piece of butter on top of each
scallop.
Bake until nicely browned.
Chopped parsley should be strewn over the fish before serving.

Homemade Toffee

Ingredients

1 lb of brown sugar
¼ lb butter
Lemon or vanilla

Method

Mix in a shallow vessel the brown sugar and butter.
Stir these well for 15 minutes or until the mixture becomes brittle when dropped into water.
Add lemon or vanilla before the cooking is complete.
Butter a fine plate.
Pour the toffee on it to cool.
When partly cold mark it off in squares with a knife.
When cold it can be easily broken.

Mince

Ingredients

1 lb Plums
¾ lb peel scraped
1½ lb currants
1 lb sultanas
1½ apples scraped, (Wellingtons)
The juice and rind of 2 lemons
1 lb demeria sugar
3 good teaspoonfuls spice
1 good teaspoonful nutmeg
Tablespoonful of whiskey

Method

Chop and peel the plums into small pieces.
Add all other ingredients and mix well.

Scotch Eggs

Ingredients

1 lb sausage meat
6 good sized eggs
Breadcrumbs.

Method

Hard boil the eggs, put them into cold water, take off the shells.
Cover well with sausage meat and roll them in the breadcrumbs.
Have ready a pan of boiling fat and fry till a nice brown.
When cold cut in halves.
Tomatoes, beetroot or parsley may be used to accompany the dish.

Surprise Sausages

Take the required number of sausages, divide each in half and remove the skin.

Roll in mashed potatoes then dip in beaten egg and coat with bread raspings.

Fry in boiling fat until crisp and brown.

Serve very hot and garnish with parsley.

Tip:
Bread Raspings = (Bread crumbs baked in oven until brown)

Lemon Curd

This recipe was given to Isabella by her Sister-in-Law, Sadie.

Ingredients

1 - 2 lumps sugar
3 eggs
3 ozs butter
2 lemons

Method

Put sugar and butter in saucepan.
Add the juice of lemons and melt a little.
Beat the eggs and add to mixture stirring until it thickens, but do not boil.

Savoury Dishes

Cheese Pudding

Ingredients

Bread
Butter
Grated or sliced cheese
½ pint milk
1 egg

Method

Butter a pie dish and put in it alternate layers of bread and butter and the cheese grated or sliced.
Whisk the egg in and pour over the dish.
Allow it to stand so that the bread is quite soaked.
Then bake in a gentle oven until well browned.
Use a baking tin for the purpose.

Sausage Rolls

Ingredients

Thick sausages
Rough Puff Pastry
Beaten egg

Method

Prick and cook half pound of thick sausages for 3 to 4 minutes in
boiling water.
Then skin and cut them across and lengthwise.
Cut thinly rolled rough puff pastry into squares of 3½ ins and in them
enclose the sausage moistening and sealing the joins but leaving the
ends open.
Brush over with beaten egg before baking in a fairly hot oven until
browned.

Macaroni Pie

Ingredients

6 ozs of macaroni
Salted water
½ oz dripping
½ oz flour
1 teaspoonful of curry powder
½ pint milk
3 ozs cold meat
1 Teaspoonful of chopped parsley, pepper and salt to taste

Method

Break into small pieces the macaroni.
Cook in boiling salted water till tender, drain well.
Melt the dripping in a saucepan.
Then stir into it very smoothly the flour and curry powder.
Add milk and stir the sauce till boiling.
Then add the macaroni and the cold meat, chopped finely, add
1 teaspoonful of chopped parsley, pepper and salt to taste.
Turn into a greased fireproof dish and sprinkle top with breadcrumbs.
Bake and serve hot.

Tomatoes and Cheese

Ingredients

6 tablespoonfuls of breadcrumbs
Grated cheese
2 lbs tomatoes
Salt
Pepper

Method

Mix well the breadcrumbs and the same quantity of grated cheese.
Well butter a pie dish and sprinkle the inside with a layer of crumbs and cheese.
Wash and dry the tomatoes, then slice them thickly.
Put a layer of crumbs then one of tomatoes till the dish is full.
The last layer should be of crumbs and cheese and slightly thicker than the others.
Put a few pieces of butter on the top and bake in a quick oven for 30 minutes.
For seasoning add pepper and salt.

Curried Rice

Ingredients

2 tablespoonfuls of rice
4 eggs
1 large onion
2 tablespoonfuls of curry powder
1 teaspoonful of sugar
1 teaspoonful of lemon juice
A little mushroom ketchup
Flour to make quite thick

Method

Select rice with a long grain.
Pour boiling water over it and shake it about until tender.
Drain off the water and dry the rice in a steamer while preparing the other ingredients.
Boil the eggs hard. Remove shells, cut them in halves and place them on a hot dish leaving little spaces between them.
Meanwhile the onion should have been cut in thin rounds and fried in butter.
When nicely blanched add to the other ingredients.
Smooth the flour and curry powder with ½ pint of stock.
Bring to the boil and when quite thick pour over the eggs etc and heap the rice round the dish as a border.

A Savoury Pudding

Ingredients

½ lb of dry crusts
1 large parboiled onion
3 ozs suet
2 ozs of coarse oatmeal
½ teaspoonful of baking powder
½ teaspoonful each of sage and sweet herbs
1 egg
1 cup of milk
Lard

Method

Take the dry crusts and soak them in water until soft.
Drain and squeeze dry, then beat up with a fork.
Chop up a large parboiled onion and the suet and add to the bread.
Mix together the coarse oatmeal, the baking powder and half
teaspoonful each of sage and sweet herbs.
Beat the egg well, add the cup of milk and mix into the other
ingredients.
Put a piece of lard in a tin and heat in the oven.
Pour in the mixture and allow ¾ of hour for baking in a fairly quick
oven.

Yorkshire Pudding

Ingredients

2 cupfuls of milk
2 eggs
6 tablespoonfuls of flour
1 pinch of salt
1 pinch of baking powder

Method

Sift the flour into a basin with the salt.
Stir in the milk very gradually.
Beat up the eggs and add to the batter.
When quite smooth allow this to stand for 2 hours in a cool place.
Then add the baking powder.
Pour into a well greased baking pan and bake for half hour in moderate oven.
If baked in a gas oven it may be partly baked in the top part of the oven then finally placed in the lower part of the oven underneath any joint that is being cooked.

Eggs Stuffed with Shrimps

Ingredients
Eggs
Little butter
Fresh shrimps
Green parsley

Method

Boil until quite hard as many eggs as are required.
Take them out of the water and allow them to get cold.
Shell eggs then cut off the top an inch down and remove the yolks without breaking the whites.
Take a nick off the bottom to allow the eggs to stand.
Fill the hollow part with the following mixture.
Mash the yolks with a little butter.
Then cut into small pieces some fresh shrimps already skinned.
Mince a little green parsley.
Mix all together.
With this fill the eggs.
Lay the cut off tops of the whites upon each and garnish with parsley before serving.

Fish Patties

Ingredients

½ lb of cold fish
Hard boiled egg
½ a teacupful of boiled rice
1 dessert spoon of finely chopped parsley
Pepper and salt
½ pint white sauce
½ lb cooked potatoes
Flour and dripping

Method

Remove all bones from the cold fish.
Chop up the hard boiled egg and add this to the fish.
Add the boiled rice, a dessert spoon of finely chopped parsley and pepper and salt to taste.
Mix all well together.
Make white sauce and add to the other ingredients.
Mash ½ lb cooked potatoes and sufficient flour and dripping to make a nice pastry.
Roll out and line some saucers with this, then fill with the mixture.
Bake till brown after covering with the rest of the pastry.

Tip:
Parsley Sauce - Never chop parsley when it is intended for sauce. Pick it from the stalk and place in a cupful of boiling water to which a pinch of soda and salt have been added. Remove the parsley and drop it into melted butter you would use for sauce.

Ham and Beef Pie

Ingredients

1½ lbs of beefsteak
½ lb ham (cooked)
4 hard boiled eggs
Chopped parsley
Chopped thyme
Lemon peel
Pepper and salt
Cupful of good stock
Rich pie-crust
1 egg

Method

Cut the beefsteak into neat pieces.
Cut the ham and the hard boiled eggs into slices.
Arrange these ingredients into layers in a pie dish.
Season each with the chopped parsley, thyme, lemon peel, pepper and salt.
Put the stock into the dish.
Cover with a rich pie-crust ornament with leaves cut out of the pastry.
Brush over the crust with beaten yolk of egg and bake in a sharp oven till the pastry is cooked.
Then let the meat cook slowly till done.
This pie is best served cold.

Bread and Cheese Savoury

Ingredients

Bread and butter
1 egg
½ pint milk
6 ozs cheese

Method

Cut the bread into slices and butter them.
Lay them in a pie dish with grated or sliced cheese in between.
Beat the egg in the milk and then pour over.
About 1½ hours required for baking.

Ham Omelette

Ingredients

3 eggs
1 tablespoonful of cream or milk
A pinch of white pepper
2 ozs cooked lean ham
1 tablespoonful of butter

Method

Break the eggs into a basin.
Add the cream or milk and the pinch of white pepper.
Beat up thoroughly.
Chop up finely the lean ham.
Melt one tablespoonful of butter in an omelette pan.
When hot put in the chopped ham and fry for a few seconds.
Blend the ham with the butter.
Pour in the beaten eggs etc and commence stirring with a fork slowly over a bright and brisk fire.
When the mixture begins to get firm fold the omelette into the shape of an oval cushion.

Sweet Puddings

Scotch Apple Pie

Ingredients

1 Dozen green apples
1 Cup full of sugar
Hand full of raisins
Half a lemon

Method

Peel the apples, cut them into quarters and remove core.
Place them in a deep pie dish.
Sprinkle over a cupful of sugar and a good handful of raisins.
Place half a lemon cut in slices on the tops.
Cover with good short pastry, brush with beaten egg and bake in moderate oven for 40 minutes.

Apple Charlottes

Recipe 1

Ingredients

2 lbs flour
1 lb butter or margarine
½ lb caster sugar
3 eggs

Method

Rub the butter and sugar together add the eggs, rub them in then draw the flour in and make the whole up to a paste without any other liquor.

Recipe 2

Ingredients

2 lbs of flour
½ oz cream of tartar
¼ oz bicarbonate of soda
1 lb margarine
½ lb caster sugar
2 eggs
A little milk

Method

Mix the chemicals in the flour. Rub the margarine in finely.
Make a hollow. Put the sugar in. Add the beaten eggs and a little milk.
Mix up to a paste. Let it stand a little while before using it.
Roll out either of the pastes. Cut out rounds with a cutter and place them in crinkled patty tins. Fill with slices of apple add a little sugar, nutmeg or cinnamon. Cut more rounds out, wet them and place them on the tops.
Pinch well all round the edges. Make a hole in the centre of each and bake in a hot oven. Dredge with sugar after baking.

Tip:
'Chemicals' = Bicarbonate of Soda and Cream of Tartar

Lemon Tart

Recipe 1.

Ingredients

1 tablespoonful of butter
1 teacupful of powdered sugar
3 eggs
Juice and grated rind of 2 lemons

Method 1

Having beaten to a cream the butter and powdered sugar, add the well beaten yolks of the eggs.

Then add the juice and grated rind of the lemons.

Beat all together then stir in lightly the whites of the eggs, beaten to a froth.

Line the dish with a light paste and bake in a quick oven.

Recipe 2.

Ingredients

1 tablespoonful of butter
1 teacupful of powdered sugar
3 eggs
Juice and grated rind of 2 lemons
Plus:
Lemons
Cupful Golden Syrup

Method 2

After lining a pie dish with pastry fill with the lemons, peeled and cut in thin slices.

(Removing every bit of the white, tough peel and seeds).

Then pour over the golden syrup.

Cover with more pastry and cook in a moderate oven.

When the pastry is brown the tart is quite ready.

Cottage Pudding

Ingredients

¼ cup butter
¼ cup sugar
1¼ cup flour
1 cup milk
1 teaspoon of carbonate of soda
1 tablespoonful of baking powder

Method

Mix the butter and sugar together until like thick cream.
Sift the soda and baking powder into the flour.
Add the milk and flour alternately to the sugar and butter.
Turn the mixture into a well greased baking tin.
Bake in a quick oven for 10 to 15 minutes.
Then cut into squares and serve with lemon sauce.

Rhubarb Turnovers

Ingredients

Pastry
Rhubarb
Sugar
Ground ginger

Method

Make some good pastry and roll it out to the thickness of a ¼ in.
Stamp it out in rounds from 4 to 6 inches in diameter and lay upon
half of the pastry a little rhubarb, cut small.
Add sugar to taste and sprinkle a little ground ginger over the fruit.
Turn the pastry over pinch the edges close together and brush with
white of egg.
Sprinkle sugar over them and bake in brisk oven for twenty minutes.

Raisin Pudding

Ingredients

12 ozs finely chopped suet
1 lb stoned raisins
4 tablespoonfuls of baked and grounded breadcrumbs.
3 tablespoonfuls of flour
5 tablespoonfuls of sugar
2 ozs chopped candied citrus peel
Grated nutmeg
Little salt
3 eggs
Milk
2 tablespoonfuls of brandy

Method

Place in a basin the finely chopped suet, stoned raisins and the baked and grounded breadcrumbs.
Then add the flour and sugar.
Mix in the chopped candied citrus peel, grated nutmeg and a little salt.
Beat the eggs well and mix with enough milk to make the ingredients into a thick batter.
Then add the brandy.
Butter a mould well.
Cover with buttered paper and steam for 4 hours.

Tip:
'Mould' (Dish or bowl of any shape which can be steamed)

Gooseberry Batter Pudding

Ingredients

Gooseberries
2 eggs
½ lb flour
1 pint milk
Brown sugar

Method

Grease a large baking tin.
Cover the bottom with gooseberries and pour over them a batter.
Batter. (Mix together the eggs, flour and milk).
The baking should take ½ hour and then the pudding can be turned out on a hot dish.
Cut into pieces of any size and serve with brown sugar.

Strawberry Trifle

Ingredients

Stale sponge cakes
1½ lb strawberries
Sugar
Water
½ pint cream

Method

Line the bottom of a glass dish with stale sponge cakes cut in slices.
Remove the stalks from strawberries, reserving ½ oz with stalks for decoration.
Make a syrup of the sugar and water and place the berries in a few at a time taking care they are not broken.
After each few have been in a couple of minutes, remove them to the dish of cakes and put more fruit into the syrup.
When all are done pour the syrup over them and leave until cold.
Whip the cream.
Add sugar to taste and pour over the strawberries.
Use the un-cooked berries for decorating the top of the trifle.

Tip:
When soaking fruit pies or tarts before putting in the fruit brush over the lining of pastry with milk. This causes the flour to cling together and the juices will not run out.

Apple Shortcake

Ingredients

2 ozs flour + 1 lb flour
Pinch salt
2 tablespoonfuls of baking powder
½ pint milk
4 large apples
2 ozs of sugar
1 oz butter
Nutmeg

Method

Rub the 2 ½ ozs of flour into the pound of flour with a pinch of salt and the baking powder and make into a paste with about half a pint of milk.
Divide it in two and roll it out into large rounds of equal size and thickness.
Put one round on a floured baking sheet.
Peel, core and slice the apples and pile them on the pastry together with the sugar and butter and a little nutmeg.
Wet the edges of the pastry, lay the other round on top.
Pinch the edges together and put it at once to bake in a hot oven.
When the pastry begins to colour remove it to a cooler part of the oven or cover it with paper and bake for thirty to forty minutes.
Before serving sift sugar on top.

Fried Apple Pastries

Ingredients

Short crust pastry
1 lb Apples
Grated rind of a lemon
4 ozs sugar

Method

Roll out and cut in rounds quantity of short crust pastry.
Peel, core and chop the apples.
Mix with them the grated rind of the lemon and the sugar.
Put a little in the centre of each round of pastry.
Wet the edges fold over and fry in very hot fat.
When brown remove from pan and drain on paper.
Serve hot after the pastry has been sifted over with castor sugar.

Bread and Raisin Pudding

Ingredients

Halved raisins
Bread
Butter
Sugar
Custard

Method

Place rows of halved raisins across the bottom and sides of a buttered basin.

Then insert layers of the thin bread and butter and between each layer place stoned raisins and a sprinkling of sugar.

When nearly full pour in enough custard to reach the top of basin.

Allow the pudding to stand for 2 hours then steam (not boil) slowly for one hour.

Macaroni Fritters

Ingredients

2 ozs macaroni
2 ozs tomatoes
1 egg
Butter
Breadcrumbs
Seasoning

Method

Boil the macaroni in salted water until quite soft.
In another pan cook tomatoes well seasoned with pepper and salt then add the butter.
When these are nearly cooked strain the water from the macaroni and drain on a cloth.
Chop up into small pieces then mash the tomatoes and mix with the macaroni.
Add sufficient breadcrumbs with the other ingredients to make the mixture stiff enough to form into cakes.
Beat up the egg on a plate roll each fritter or flat cake in the egg.
Then put carefully into a pan of hot butter or frying fat.
They will be ready when fried brown.

Whole Apples Stewed

Ingredients

Several apples
Sugar
Cloves
Water
Breadcrumbs and custard

Method

Peel and core several apples.
Arrange in a flat saucepan.
Fill the cavities of the apples with sugar and put a clove in each.
Add water to the depth of a couple of inches.
Cook until tender adding more water if necessary and then remove the apples to a serving dish.
Cook the syrup until it is thick then pour it over the apples.
Breadcrumbs and custard should be served with the dish.

Baked Apples with Raisins

Ingredients

Several large round apples
Seedless raisins
Water
½ cupful of sugar per 6 apples

Method

Core the apples and place in baking tin.
Fill the cavities made by the core half full with the seedless raisins.
Cover the bottom of the pan with water and bake until soft in a quick oven.
Take the sugar and make a syrup of the juice remaining in the pan.
Add more water if necessary.
Pour over the apples.
Eat cold.

Chocolate Mould

Ingredients

2 ozs cornflour
2 ozs cocoa
Cold milk
Sweet milk
Heaped tablespoonful of sugar
Vanilla or lemon

Method

Take the cornflour and cocoa.
After mixing these together blend with a little cold milk.
Put a pint of good sweet milk in a saucepan.
Add the sugar and boil.
Now stir the cornflour and cocoa mixture into the boiling milk.
Simmer for 7 minutes.
Flavour with the vanilla or lemon and pour into a mould.
Rinse out the mould with cold water before pouring in the mixture.

Tip:
Sweet Milk = (tin condensed milk)

Ginger Pudding and Sweet Sauce

Ingredients

¾ lb flour
¼ lb of soaked bread
6 ozs suet
½ lb treacle
½ oz ginger
2 ozs sugar
1 teaspoonful of baking powder
Pinch of salt
¼ pint milk
Sauce
1 pint of water
1 oz cornflour
1 oz sugar
Flavouring if desired

Method

Mix the flour, ginger, baking powder and salt.
Add the suet finely chopped and the soaked bread (well drained).
Melt the syrup by slightly warming it.
Mix it with the milk and add these to the dry ingredients.
Mix all thoroughly and place in a greased tin or basin.
Cover it with a plate or greased paper and steam for 2 hours.
Turn the pudding out and serve hot with sauce.

Sauce:
Mix the cornflour to a smooth paste with a little of the water.
Boil the rest of the water.
Stir in the cornflour, sugar and flavouring.
Boil up and cook for about 3 minutes.

Stewed Apples

Pick out apples of equal size.
Wash and peel them, stalk each and put them into a
saucepan of water with a slice of lemon.
Allow them to stew until tender.
Should the water boil away add more.
Then put on dish with a little of the liquor and serve
with castor sugar.

Xmas Pudding

Ingredients

1 lb Peel
1 lb Sultanas
1 lb Plums (Dried Prunes are easier) (cut into small pieces)
1½ lbs currants
½ lb flour (Plain)
½ lb best beef suet (kidney)
1 lb Demerara Sugar
½ lb breadcrumbs
1½ lbs apples (Wellingtons)
6 eggs
¼ pint old ale
3 teaspoonfuls spice
1 teaspoonful nutmeg
Rind and juice of 2 lemons

Method

Mix all ingredients together.
Make dough for basins. Boil 10 hours.

Tip:

Dough = (not provided) (dough made from flour and water) you will need to find a recipe. Once made this was put on top of Pudding. (This was instead of cloth or greased paper as used today).

Steamed Lemon Pudding

Ingredients

6 ozs Self raising flour
3 ozs Margarine
2 eggs
4 ozs castor sugar
1 grated rind of lemon (only rind)

Method

Mix together Margarine and the sugar.
Beat in the eggs.
Add lemon rind.
Fold in the flour.
Put jam at bottom of basin.
Steam for 2 hours.

Lemon Pudding
Baked later

Ingredients

Sliced bread
Milk
Knob margarine
Sugar
2 egg yokes beaten up
Rind and juice of 1 lemon

Method

Soak the bread in the milk.
Add some sugar.
Beat egg yokes and add.
Add rind and juice of lemon.
Put in oven lightly brown.
Whisk the egg whites.
Place on top and put back in oven to lightly brown.

Lemon Curd

This recipe was given to Isabella by her Sister-in-Law, Sadie.

Ingredients

1 - 2 lumps of sugar
3 eggs
3 ozs butter
2 lemons

Method

Put sugar and butter in saucepan.
Add the juice of lemons and melt a little.
Beat the eggs and add to mixture stirring until it thickens, but do not boil.

Prune Pudding

Ingredients

3 ozs of beef suet
6 ozs of fine breadcrumbs
½ lb prunes
½ a teaspoonful of cinnamon,
2 tablespoonfuls of sugar
2 eggs

Method

After chopping finely the beef suet, mix in lightly the fine
breadcrumbs.
Remove the stones from the prunes.
Cut each one in 4 pieces.
Mix them with the suet and breadcrumbs.
Add the cinnamon, sugar and eggs.
Beat all together with a fork until it is moist but not wet.
Put the mixture into a well greased bowl, tie a cloth over and boil for
1 hour and half.

Decorated Apple Charlotte

Ingredients

Apples
Fine breadcrumbs
Sugar
1 egg white
3 ozs of sugar

Method

For these use round or oval cake tins.
Line them with either of the Charlotte pasties tins.
Place the fine breadcrumbs at the bottom of each one.
Place some apple slices inside and a little sugar.
Cover them over with a sheet of paper and bake in a hot oven.
This prevents the apples from burning before the paste is set.
When they are done beat up the egg white with the sugar.
Spread it over the apples.
Put back in the oven to brown, then dredge with sugar.

Tip:
Paper! May be better to use tinfoil!

Baked Gooseberry Pudding

Ingredients

A quart gooseberries
Butter
Sugar
Breadcrumbs
Custard

Method

Stew the gooseberries to a pulp.
Put them through a sieve.
Add a piece of butter, some more sugar and sufficient fine
breadcrumbs to make the mixture quite stiff.
Put into a buttered pudding dish.
Fill up the dish with custard and bake until lightly browned.

Tip:
1 Quart = 2 pints

Marmalade Pudding

Ingredients

Bread
Butter
Powdered Sugar
Marmalade
Half teacupful of new milk
1 pint custard (home made)

Method

Slice a quantity of bread which is not very stale and cut the crusts off.
Nearly fill a pie dish.
Each slice should be spread with butter and sprinkled with the
powdered sugar.
Butter the pie dish and lay in the bread and butter and spread the
marmalade over each layer.
In order to moisten the bread pour half teacupful of new milk over
these ingredients.
Then make a pint of custard and while hot gently pour in dish.
Bake for half hour.

Batter Pudding

Ingredients

4 ozs flour
1 teaspoonful of baking powder
A small quantity sugar
1 egg
Milk
Currants

Method

Mix all the ingredients with milk until they become a thin batter.
Then bake in a well buttered tin in a brisk oven for ½ hour.
If preferred a few currants may be stewed at the bottom of the tin.
Will convey additional flavour.

Lemon Pudding

Ingredients

Lemon
1 oz of cornflour
Cold water
2 ozs sugar
1 egg
Crust pastry
1 oz butter

Method

Take the rind of the lemon, grate it and squeeze out all the juice.
Make a smooth paste with the cornflour and cold water.
Pour it into a cupful of boiling water and stir till thickened.
Add the juice strained and grated rind of the lemon to the sugar and the egg, beat well.
Line a pie dish with pastry.
Pour in the mixture.
Cover with more crust and bake till ready about ¾ hours or longer.
If thought desirable add 1 oz butter to the mixture.

A Savoury Pudding

Ingredients

½ lb of dry crusts
1 large parboiled onion
3 ozs suet
2 ozs of coarse oatmeal
½ teaspoonful of baking powder
½ teaspoonful each of sage and sweet herbs
1 egg
1 cup of milk
Lard

Method

Take the dry crusts and soak them in water until soft.
Drain and squeeze dry, then beat up with a fork.
Chop up a large parboiled onion and the suet and add to the bread.
Mix together the coarse oatmeal, the baking powder and half teaspoonful each of sage and sweet herbs.
Beat the egg well, add the cup of milk and mix into the other ingredients.
Put a piece of lard in a tin and heat in the oven.
Pour in the mixture and allow ¾ of hour for baking in a fairly quick oven.

Index